WAINWRIGHT'S
DESTRUCTIBLE
COLOURABLE
FLASHCARDABLE

TOP 30 DOODLE QUOTATION GUIDE
TO
AN INSPECTOR CALLS
BY
J B PRIESTLEY

QUOTATIONS CHOSEN AND DRAWN BY EDWARD WAINWRIGHT

ISBN: 9781687269171

HOW TO ABUSE THIS VERY PRECIOUS BOOK

THIS BOOK IS MEANT TO HELP YOU TO REMEMBER USEFUL QUOTATIONS SO THAT YOU CAN USE THEM IN YOUR EXAM. TO DO THAT YOU CAN ABUSE THIS BOOK HOWEVER YOU LIKE — BUT

HERE ARE SOME IDEAS:

1. WHERE THERE ARE ALREADY DOODLES, COLOUR THEM IN— IT'S A RELAXING THING TO DO WHEN YOU'VE NO BRAIN LEFT FOR OTHER REVISION.

2. WHERE THERE ARE QUOTATIONS WITH NO DOODLE, DOODLE YOUR OWN DOODLE TO SUIT IT. DOODLE.

3. IF YOU THINK A QUOTATION IS VERY IMPORTANT, TEAR IT OUT OF THE BOOK AND STICK IT UP SOMEWHERE YOU'LL SEE IT OFTEN. SCATTER THEM AROUND THE HOUSE TO DELIGHT YOUR FAMILY.

4. SHARE YOUR BEAUTIFUL OR HILARIOUS DOODLES ONLINE— YOUR FRIENDS NEED THEM!

Can't draw? Don't worry!

There are some memorably terrible doodles in here — the important part is that they're memorable and help you to learn the quotations.

Draw, colour, share with your friends.

One more thing:

DON'T FORGET TO USE YOUR SCRIPT OF "AN
INSPECTOR CALLS" WITH THIS BOOK. ALSO, USE
A DICTIONARY OR THE INTERNET TO LOOK UP
ANY UNFAMILIAR WORDS AND WHEN YOU'VE
DONE THAT LABEL THEM, OR YOU'LL
STRUGGLE IN THE BLOOD AND FIRE
AND ANGUISH OF YOUR EXAM.

A NOTE ON THE QUOTATIONS

IF A QUOTATION IS IN SQUARE BRACKETS, IT'S A STAGE DIRECTION. FOR EXAMPLE:

[Re-enter EDNA with MACBETH's head]

STAGE DIRECTIONS ARE IMPORTANT AND SHOULD BE QUOTED — THEY TELL YOU WHAT THE PLAY SHOULD LOOK LIKE. THEY'RE VITAL!

THE INSPECTOR is not, remember, a real policeman — or man. No character is real: they are <u>all</u> symbols. THE INSPECTOR may be guilt, conscience — you decide. He is not a man.

THIS GUIDE EXISTS TO HELP YOU TO REMEMBER QUOTATIONS. IT HAS MENTIONED STAGE DIRECTIONS BECAUSE THEY MATTER TO HOW THE QUOTATIONS LOOK IN THE GUIDE.

OTHER GUIDES ARE AVAILABLE TO HELP YOU TO LEARN ABOUT TECHNIQUES AND FEATURES.

NOW, TO THE QUOTATIONS!

[The lighting should be pink and intimate until the INSPECTOR arrives, and then it should be brighter and harder]

FLASHCARD

TEAR THIS PAGE OUT, FILL THIS SIDE IN AND BINGO! YOU HAVE A FABULOUS FLASHCARD.

THIS QUOTATION IS FROM ACT _____ .

THE WORDS BELONG TO _____

_____ .

ONE LITERARY TECHNIQUE USED IS

_____ .

ANOTHER LITERARY TECHNIQUE USED IS

_____ .

THE WORD CLASS OF THE KEY WORD

" _____ " IS _____ .

WRITE THE QUOTATION HERE — MAKE SURE IT IS EXACTLY THE SAME AS IT IS ON THE OTHER SIDE !

ASK: HOW DOES THIS MAKE YOU FEEL?
ASK: HOW WOULD OTHER AUDIENCES FEEL?
ASK: HOW DOES THIS LINK TO CONTEXT?
ASK: DO OTHER QUOTATIONS LINK TO THIS?

FLASHCARD

TEAR THIS PAGE OUT, FILL THIS SIDE IN AND BINGO! YOU HAVE A FABULOUS FLASHCARD.

THIS QUOTATION IS FROM ACT _____ .

THE WORDS BELONG TO _____

_____ .

ONE LITERARY TECHNIQUE USED IS

_____

ANOTHER LITERARY TECHNIQUE USED IS

_____

THE WORD CLASS OF THE KEY WORD

" _____ " IS _____ .

WRITE THE QUOTATION HERE — MAKE SURE IT IS EXACTLY THE SAME AS IT IS ON THE OTHER SIDE !

ASK: HOW DOES THIS MAKE YOU FEEL?
ASK: HOW WOULD OTHER AUDIENCES FEEL?
ASK: HOW DOES THIS LINK TO CONTEXT?
ASK: DO OTHER QUOTATIONS LINK TO THIS?

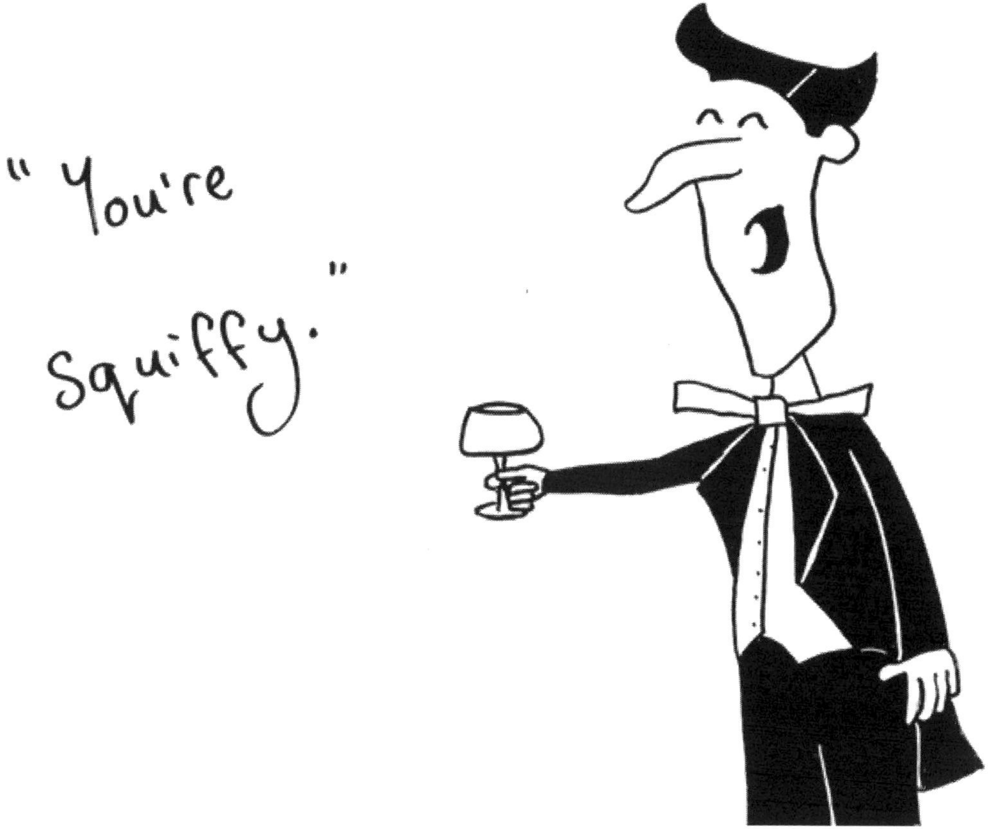
"You're squiffy."

FLASHCARD

THIS QUOTATION IS FROM ACT _____ .

THE WORDS BELONG TO _____

_____ .

ONE LITERARY TECHNIQUE USED IS

_____ .

ANOTHER LITERARY TECHNIQUE USED IS

_____ .

THE WORD CLASS OF THE KEY WORD

" _____ " IS _____ .

WRITE THE QUOTATION HERE — MAKE SURE IT IS EXACTLY THE SAME AS IT IS ON THE OTHER SIDE!

ASK: HOW DOES THIS MAKE YOU FEEL?
ASK: HOW WOULD OTHER AUDIENCES FEEL?
ASK: HOW DOES THIS LINK TO CONTEXT?
ASK: DO OTHER QUOTATIONS LINK TO THIS?

"Just a knighthood, of course."

FLASHCARD

TEAR THIS PAGE OUT, FILL THIS SIDE IN AND BINGO! YOU HAVE A FABULOUS FLASHCARD.

THIS QUOTATION IS FROM ACT _____.

THE WORDS BELONG TO _____

_____.

ONE LITERARY TECHNIQUE USED IS

_____.

ANOTHER LITERARY TECHNIQUE USED IS

_____.

THE WORD CLASS OF THE KEY WORD

" _____ " IS _____.

WRITE THE QUOTATION HERE — MAKE SURE IT IS EXACTLY THE SAME AS IT IS ON THE OTHER SIDE!

ASK: HOW DOES THIS MAKE YOU FEEL?
ASK: HOW WOULD OTHER AUDIENCES FEEL?
ASK: HOW DOES THIS LINK TO CONTEXT?
ASK: DO OTHER QUOTATIONS LINK TO THIS?

[He creates at once an impression of Massiveness, Solidity and purposefulness]

FLASHCARD

TEAR THIS PAGE OUT, FILL THIS SIDE IN AND BINGO! YOU HAVE A FABULOUS FLASHCARD.

THIS QUOTATION IS FROM ACT _____.

THE WORDS BELONG TO _____

_____.

ONE LITERARY TECHNIQUE USED IS

_____.

ANOTHER LITERARY TECHNIQUE USED IS

_____.

THE WORD CLASS OF THE KEY WORD

" _____ " IS _____.

WRITE THE QUOTATION HERE — MAKE SURE IT IS <u>EXACTLY</u> THE SAME AS IT IS ON THE <u>OTHER</u> SIDE!

ASK: HOW DOES THIS MAKE YOU FEEL?

ASK: HOW WOULD OTHER AUDIENCES FEEL?

ASK: HOW DOES THIS LINK TO CONTEXT?

ASK: DO OTHER QUOTATIONS LINK TO THIS?

"Burnt her inside out, of course."

FLASHCARD

TEAR THIS PAGE OUT, FILL THIS SIDE IN AND BINGO! YOU HAVE A FABULOUS FLASHCARD.

THIS QUOTATION IS FROM ACT _____ .

THE WORDS BELONG TO _____

_____ .

ONE LITERARY TECHNIQUE USED IS

_____ .

ANOTHER LITERARY TECHNIQUE USED IS

_____ .

THE WORD CLASS OF THE KEY WORD

" _____ " IS _____ .

WRITE THE QUOTATION HERE — MAKE SURE IT IS EXACTLY THE SAME AS IT IS ON THE OTHER SIDE!

ASK: HOW DOES THIS MAKE YOU FEEL?
ASK: HOW WOULD OTHER AUDIENCES FEEL?
ASK: HOW DOES THIS LINK TO CONTEXT?
ASK: DO OTHER QUOTATIONS LINK TO THIS?

"If we were all responsible for everything that happened to everybody we'd had anything to do with, it would be very awkward, wouldn't it?"

FLASHCARD

TEAR THIS PAGE OUT, FILL THIS SIDE IN AND BINGO! YOU HAVE A FABULOUS FLASHCARD.

THIS QUOTATION IS FROM ACT _____.

THE WORDS BELONG TO _____

_____.

ONE LITERARY TECHNIQUE USED IS

_____

ANOTHER LITERARY TECHNIQUE USED IS

_____

THE WORD CLASS OF THE KEY WORD

" _____ " IS _____.

WRITE THE QUOTATION HERE — MAKE SURE IT IS EXACTLY THE SAME AS IT IS ON THE OTHER SIDE!

ASK: HOW DOES THIS MAKE YOU FEEL?
ASK: HOW WOULD OTHER AUDIENCES FEEL?
ASK: HOW DOES THIS LINK TO CONTEXT?
ASK: DO OTHER QUOTATIONS LINK TO THIS?

"It's better to ask for the Earth than to take it."

FLASHCARD

TEAR THIS PAGE OUT, FILL THIS SIDE IN AND BINGO! YOU HAVE A FABULOUS FLASHCARD.

THIS QUOTATION IS FROM ACT _____ .

THE WORDS BELONG TO _____

_____

ONE LITERARY TECHNIQUE USED IS

_____

ANOTHER LITERARY TECHNIQUE USED IS

_____

THE WORD CLASS OF THE KEY WORD

" _____ " IS _____ .

WRITE THE QUOTATION HERE — MAKE SURE IT IS EXACTLY THE SAME AS IT IS ON THE OTHER SIDE!

ASK: HOW DOES THIS MAKE YOU FEEL?
ASK: HOW WOULD OTHER AUDIENCES FEEL?
ASK: HOW DOES THIS LINK TO CONTEXT?
ASK: DO OTHER QUOTATIONS LINK TO THIS?

FLASHCARD

TEAR THIS PAGE OUT, FILL THIS SIDE IN AND BINGO! YOU HAVE A FABULOUS FLASHCARD.

THIS QUOTATION IS FROM ACT _____.

THE WORDS BELONG TO _____

_____.

ONE LITERARY TECHNIQUE USED IS

_____.

ANOTHER LITERARY TECHNIQUE USED IS

_____.

THE WORD CLASS OF THE KEY WORD

" _____ " IS _____.

WRITE THE QUOTATION HERE — MAKE SURE IT IS EXACTLY THE SAME AS IT IS ON THE OTHER SIDE!

ASK: HOW DOES THIS MAKE YOU FEEL?
ASK: HOW WOULD OTHER AUDIENCES FEEL?
ASK: HOW DOES THIS LINK TO CONTEXT?
ASK: DO OTHER QUOTATIONS LINK TO THIS?

"All right.
I knew her.
Let's leave
it at that."

FLASHCARD

TEAR THIS PAGE OUT, FILL THIS SIDE IN AND BINGO! YOU HAVE A FABULOUS FLASHCARD.

THIS QUOTATION IS FROM ACT _____.

THE WORDS BELONG TO _____

_____.

ONE LITERARY TECHNIQUE USED IS

_____.

ANOTHER LITERARY TECHNIQUE USED IS

_____.

THE WORD CLASS OF THE KEY WORD

" _____ " IS _____ .

WRITE THE QUOTATION HERE — MAKE SURE IT IS EXACTLY THE SAME AS IT IS ON THE OTHER SIDE!

ASK: HOW DOES THIS MAKE YOU FEEL?

ASK: HOW WOULD OTHER AUDIENCES FEEL?

ASK: HOW DOES THIS LINK TO CONTEXT?

ASK: DO OTHER QUOTATIONS LINK TO THIS?

"She feels responsible."

FLASHCARD

TEAR THIS PAGE OUT, FILL THIS SIDE IN AND BINGO! YOU HAVE A FABULOUS FLASHCARD.

THIS QUOTATION IS FROM ACT _____ .

THE WORDS BELONG TO _____

_____ .

ONE LITERARY TECHNIQUE USED IS

_____ .

ANOTHER LITERARY TECHNIQUE USED IS

_____ .

THE WORD CLASS OF THE KEY WORD

" _____ " IS _____ .

WRITE THE QUOTATION HERE — MAKE SURE IT IS EXACTLY THE SAME AS IT IS ON THE OTHER SIDE!

ASK: HOW DOES THIS MAKE YOU FEEL?
ASK: HOW WOULD OTHER AUDIENCES FEEL?
ASK: HOW DOES THIS LINK TO CONTEXT?
ASK: DO OTHER QUOTATIONS LINK TO THIS?

"You mustn't try to build up a kind of wall between us and that girl."

FLASHCARD

TEAR THIS PAGE OUT, FILL THIS SIDE IN AND BINGO! YOU HAVE A FABULOUS FLASHCARD.

THIS QUOTATION IS FROM ACT _____ .

THE WORDS BELONG TO _____

_____ .

ONE LITERARY TECHNIQUE USED IS

_____ .

ANOTHER LITERARY TECHNIQUE USED IS

_____ .

THE WORD CLASS OF THE KEY WORD

" _____ " IS _____ .

WRITE THE QUOTATION HERE — MAKE SURE IT IS <u>EXACTLY</u> THE SAME AS IT IS ON THE OTHER SIDE!

ASK: HOW DOES THIS MAKE YOU FEEL?
ASK: HOW WOULD OTHER AUDIENCES FEEL?
ASK: HOW DOES THIS LINK TO CONTEXT?
ASK: DO OTHER QUOTATIONS LINK TO THIS?

FLASHCARD

THIS QUOTATION IS FROM ACT _____.

THE WORDS BELONG TO _____

_____.

ONE LITERARY TECHNIQUE USED IS

_____.

ANOTHER LITERARY TECHNIQUE USED IS

_____.

THE WORD CLASS OF THE KEY WORD

" _____ " IS _____.

WRITE THE QUOTATION HERE — MAKE SURE IT IS EXACTLY THE SAME AS IT IS ON THE OTHER SIDE!

ASK: HOW DOES THIS MAKE YOU FEEL?
ASK: HOW WOULD OTHER AUDIENCES FEEL?
ASK: HOW DOES THIS LINK TO CONTEXT?
ASK: DO OTHER QUOTATIONS LINK TO THIS?

"It's a favourite haunt of the women of the town."

FLASHCARD

TEAR THIS PAGE OUT, FILL THIS SIDE IN AND BINGO! YOU HAVE A FABULOUS FLASHCARD.

THIS QUOTATION IS FROM ACT _____.

THE WORDS BELONG TO _____

_____

ONE LITERARY TECHNIQUE USED IS

_____

ANOTHER LITERARY TECHNIQUE USED IS

_____

THE WORD CLASS OF THE KEY WORD

" _____ " IS _____.

WRITE THE QUOTATION HERE — MAKE SURE IT IS <u>EXACTLY</u> THE SAME AS IT IS ON THE OTHER SIDE!

ASK: HOW DOES THIS MAKE YOU FEEL?
ASK: HOW WOULD OTHER AUDIENCES FEEL?
ASK: HOW DOES THIS LINK TO CONTEXT?
ASK: DO OTHER QUOTATIONS LINK TO THIS?

BRUMLEY WOMEN'S CHARITY

APPEAL FOR AID FORM

NAME: Mrs Birling.

CASE: Mrs Birling 12:00

REQUIREMENTS: Unemployed

Single Mother's Support.

~~DESERVING~~ ☐

Most UNDESERVING ☒ impertinent

SIGNED: Mrs Birling

POSITION: Chair ⏱ 12:00

"I didn't like her manner. She'd impertinently made use of our name."

FLASHCARD

TEAR THIS PAGE OUT, FILL THIS SIDE IN AND BINGO! YOU HAVE A FABULOUS FLASHCARD.

THIS QUOTATION IS FROM ACT _____ .

THE WORDS BELONG TO _____

_____ .

ONE LITERARY TECHNIQUE USED IS

_____ .

ANOTHER LITERARY TECHNIQUE USED IS

_____ .

THE WORD CLASS OF THE KEY WORD

" _____ " IS _____ .

WRITE THE QUOTATION HERE — MAKE SURE IT IS EXACTLY THE SAME AS IT IS ON THE OTHER SIDE!

ASK: HOW DOES THIS MAKE YOU FEEL?

ASK: HOW WOULD OTHER AUDIENCES FEEL?

ASK: HOW DOES THIS LINK TO CONTEXT?

ASK: DO OTHER QUOTATIONS LINK TO THIS?

"I think you did something terribly wrong — and that you're going to spend the rest of your life regretting it."

FLASHCARD

THIS QUOTATION IS FROM ACT _____.

THE WORDS BELONG TO _____

_____.

ONE LITERARY TECHNIQUE USED IS

_____.

ANOTHER LITERARY TECHNIQUE USED IS

_____.

THE WORD CLASS OF THE KEY WORD

" _____ " IS _____.

WRITE THE QUOTATION HERE — MAKE SURE IT IS EXACTLY THE SAME AS IT IS ON THE OTHER SIDE!

ASK: HOW DOES THIS MAKE YOU FEEL?

ASK: HOW WOULD OTHER AUDIENCES FEEL?

ASK: HOW DOES THIS LINK TO CONTEXT?

ASK: DO OTHER QUOTATIONS LINK TO THIS?

FLASHCARD

TEAR THIS PAGE OUT, FILL THIS SIDE IN AND BINGO! YOU HAVE A FABULOUS FLASHCARD.

THIS QUOTATION IS FROM ACT _____.

THE WORDS BELONG TO _____

_____.

ONE LITERARY TECHNIQUE USED IS

_____.

ANOTHER LITERARY TECHNIQUE USED IS

_____.

THE WORD CLASS OF THE KEY WORD

" _____ " IS _____.

WRITE THE QUOTATION HERE — MAKE SURE IT IS EXACTLY THE SAME AS IT IS ON THE OTHER SIDE!

ASK: HOW DOES THIS MAKE YOU FEEL?
ASK: HOW WOULD OTHER AUDIENCES FEEL?
ASK: HOW DOES THIS LINK TO CONTEXT?
ASK: DO OTHER QUOTATIONS LINK TO THIS?

"You little sneak."

FLASHCARD

TEAR THIS PAGE OUT, FILL THIS SIDE IN AND BINGO! YOU HAVE A FABULOUS FLASHCARD.

THIS QUOTATION IS FROM ACT _____.

THE WORDS BELONG TO _____

_____.

ONE LITERARY TECHNIQUE USED IS

_____.

ANOTHER LITERARY TECHNIQUE USED IS

_____.

THE WORD CLASS OF THE KEY WORD

" _____ " IS _____.

WRITE THE QUOTATION HERE — MAKE SURE IT IS <u>EXACTLY</u> THE SAME AS IT IS ON THE OTHER SIDE!

ASK: HOW DOES THIS MAKE YOU FEEL?
ASK: HOW WOULD OTHER AUDIENCES FEEL?
ASK: HOW DOES THIS LINK TO CONTEXT?
ASK: DO OTHER QUOTATIONS LINK TO THIS?

"She didn't want me to go in."

FLASHCARD

THIS QUOTATION IS FROM ACT _____ .

THE WORDS BELONG TO _____

_____ .

ONE LITERARY TECHNIQUE USED IS

_____ .

ANOTHER LITERARY TECHNIQUE USED IS

_____ .

THE WORD CLASS OF THE KEY WORD

" _____ " IS _____ .

WRITE THE QUOTATION HERE — MAKE SURE IT IS <u>EXACTLY</u> THE SAME AS IT IS ON THE OTHER SIDE!

ASK: HOW DOES THIS MAKE YOU FEEL?
ASK: HOW WOULD OTHER AUDIENCES FEEL?
ASK: HOW DOES THIS LINK TO CONTEXT?
ASK: DO OTHER QUOTATIONS LINK TO THIS?

"Then – you killed her... and the child she'd have had too – my child – your own grandchild – you killed them both – damn you, damn you – "

FLASHCARD

TEAR THIS PAGE OUT, FILL THIS SIDE IN AND BINGO! YOU HAVE A FABULOUS FLASHCARD.

THIS QUOTATION IS FROM ACT _____ .

THE WORDS BELONG TO _____

_____ .

ONE LITERARY TECHNIQUE USED IS

_____ .

ANOTHER LITERARY TECHNIQUE USED IS

_____ .

THE WORD CLASS OF THE KEY WORD

" _____ " IS _____ .

WRITE THE QUOTATION HERE — MAKE SURE IT IS EXACTLY THE SAME AS IT IS ON THE OTHER SIDE!

ASK: HOW DOES THIS MAKE YOU FEEL?

ASK: HOW WOULD OTHER AUDIENCES FEEL?

ASK: HOW DOES THIS LINK TO CONTEXT?

ASK: DO OTHER QUOTATIONS LINK TO THIS?

"There are millions and millions and millions of Eva Smiths and John Smiths still left with us."

FLASHCARD

TEAR THIS PAGE OUT, FILL THIS SIDE IN AND BINGO! YOU HAVE A FABULOUS FLASHCARD.

THIS QUOTATION IS FROM ACT _____ .

THE WORDS BELONG TO _____

_____ .

ONE LITERARY TECHNIQUE USED IS

_____ .

ANOTHER LITERARY TECHNIQUE USED IS

_____ .

THE WORD CLASS OF THE KEY WORD

" _____ " IS _____ .

WRITE THE QUOTATION HERE — MAKE SURE IT IS EXACTLY THE SAME AS IT IS ON THE OTHER SIDE!

ASK: HOW DOES THIS MAKE YOU FEEL?
ASK: HOW WOULD OTHER AUDIENCES FEEL?
ASK: HOW DOES THIS LINK TO CONTEXT?
ASK: DO OTHER QUOTATIONS LINK TO THIS?

"We don't live alone. We are members of one body. We are responsible for each other."

FLASHCARD

TEAR THIS PAGE OUT, FILL THIS SIDE IN AND BINGO! YOU HAVE A FABULOUS FLASHCARD.

THIS QUOTATION IS FROM ACT _____ .

THE WORDS BELONG TO _____

_____ .

ONE LITERARY TECHNIQUE USED IS

_____ .

ANOTHER LITERARY TECHNIQUE USED IS

_____ .

THE WORD CLASS OF THE KEY WORD

" _____ " IS _____ .

WRITE THE QUOTATION HERE — MAKE SURE IT IS <u>EXACTLY</u> THE SAME AS IT IS ON THE OTHER SIDE !

ASK: HOW DOES THIS MAKE YOU FEEL?
ASK: HOW WOULD OTHER AUDIENCES FEEL?
ASK: HOW DOES THIS LINK TO CONTEXT?
ASK: DO OTHER QUOTATIONS LINK TO THIS?

FLASHCARD

TEAR THIS PAGE OUT, FILL THIS SIDE IN AND BINGO! YOU HAVE A FABULOUS FLASHCARD.

THIS QUOTATION IS FROM ACT _____ .

THE WORDS BELONG TO _____

_____ .

ONE LITERARY TECHNIQUE USED IS

_____ .

ANOTHER LITERARY TECHNIQUE USED IS

_____ .

THE WORD CLASS OF THE KEY WORD

" _____ " IS _____ .

WRITE THE QUOTATION HERE — MAKE SURE IT IS <u>EXACTLY</u> THE SAME AS IT IS ON THE OTHER SIDE!

ASK: HOW DOES THIS MAKE YOU FEEL?
ASK: HOW WOULD OTHER AUDIENCES FEEL?
ASK: HOW DOES THIS LINK TO CONTEXT?
ASK: DO OTHER QUOTATIONS LINK TO THIS?

"You don't seem to have learnt anything."

FLASHCARD

TEAR THIS PAGE OUT, FILL THIS SIDE IN AND BINGO! YOU HAVE A FABULOUS FLASHCARD.

THIS QUOTATION IS FROM ACT _____ .

THE WORDS BELONG TO _____

_____ .

ONE LITERARY TECHNIQUE USED IS

_____ .

ANOTHER LITERARY TECHNIQUE USED IS

_____ .

THE WORD CLASS OF THE KEY WORD

" _____ " IS _____ .

WRITE THE QUOTATION HERE — MAKE SURE IT IS <u>EXACTLY</u> THE SAME AS IT IS ON THE OTHER SIDE!

ASK: HOW DOES THIS MAKE YOU FEEL?
ASK: HOW WOULD OTHER AUDIENCES FEEL?
ASK: HOW DOES THIS LINK TO CONTEXT?
ASK: DO OTHER QUOTATIONS LINK TO THIS?

"I suppose we're all nice people now."

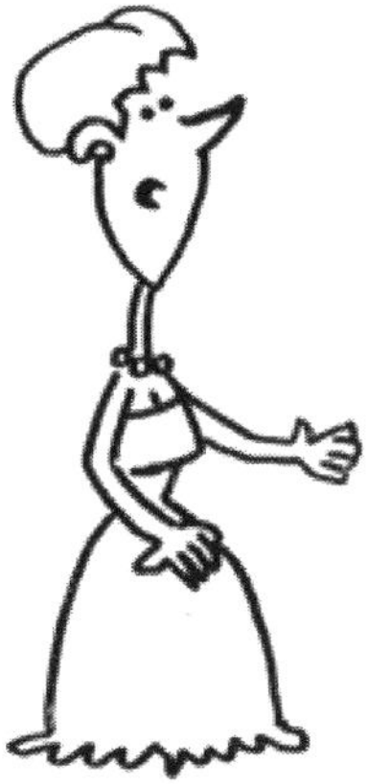

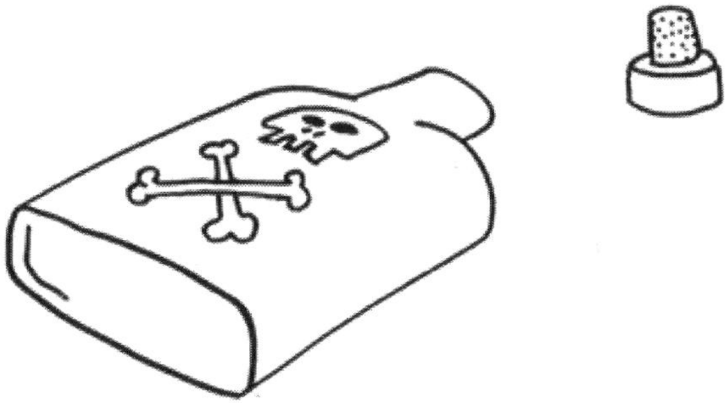

FLASHCARD

TEAR THIS PAGE OUT, FILL THIS SIDE IN AND BINGO! YOU HAVE A FABULOUS FLASHCARD.

THIS QUOTATION IS FROM ACT _____ .

THE WORDS BELONG TO _____

_____ .

ONE LITERARY TECHNIQUE USED IS

_____ .

ANOTHER LITERARY TECHNIQUE USED IS

_____ .

THE WORD CLASS OF THE KEY WORD

" _____ " IS _____ .

WRITE THE QUOTATION HERE — MAKE SURE IT IS EXACTLY THE SAME AS IT IS ON THE OTHER SIDE!

ASK: HOW DOES THIS MAKE YOU FEEL?
ASK: HOW WOULD OTHER AUDIENCES FEEL?
ASK: HOW DOES THIS LINK TO CONTEXT?
ASK: DO OTHER QUOTATIONS LINK TO THIS?

"The whole story's a lot of moonshine. Nothing but an elaborate sell!"

FLASHCARD

TEAR THIS PAGE OUT, FILL THIS SIDE IN AND BINGO! YOU HAVE A FABULOUS FLASHCARD.

THIS QUOTATION IS FROM ACT _____.

THE WORDS BELONG TO _____

_____.

ONE LITERARY TECHNIQUE USED IS

_____.

ANOTHER LITERARY TECHNIQUE USED IS

_____.

THE WORD CLASS OF THE KEY WORD

" _____ " IS _____.

WRITE THE QUOTATION HERE — MAKE SURE IT IS <u>EXACTLY</u> THE SAME AS IT IS ON THE OTHER SIDE!

ASK: HOW DOES THIS MAKE YOU FEEL?

ASK: HOW WOULD OTHER AUDIENCES FEEL?

ASK: HOW DOES THIS LINK TO CONTEXT?

ASK: DO OTHER QUOTATIONS LINK TO THIS?

"Everything we said happened really had happened."

FLASHCARD

THIS QUOTATION IS FROM ACT _____.

THE WORDS BELONG TO _____

_____.

ONE LITERARY TECHNIQUE USED IS

_____.

ANOTHER LITERARY TECHNIQUE USED IS

_____.

THE WORD CLASS OF THE KEY WORD

" _____ " IS _____.

WRITE THE QUOTATION HERE — MAKE SURE IT IS <u>EXACTLY</u> THE SAME AS IT IS ON THE <u>OTHER</u> SIDE!

ASK: HOW DOES THIS MAKE YOU FEEL?
ASK: HOW WOULD OTHER AUDIENCES FEEL?
ASK: HOW DOES THIS LINK TO CONTEXT?
ASK: DO OTHER QUOTATIONS LINK TO THIS?

"I remember what he said, how he looked, and what he made me feel. Fire and blood and anguish."

FLASHCARD

THIS QUOTATION IS FROM ACT _____.

THE WORDS BELONG TO _____

_____.

ONE LITERARY TECHNIQUE USED IS

_____.

ANOTHER LITERARY TECHNIQUE USED IS

_____.

THE WORD CLASS OF THE KEY WORD

" _____ " IS _____.

WRITE THE QUOTATION HERE — MAKE SURE IT IS <u>EXACTLY</u> THE SAME AS IT IS ON THE OTHER SIDE!

ASK: HOW DOES THIS MAKE YOU FEEL?

ASK: HOW WOULD OTHER AUDIENCES FEEL?

ASK: HOW DOES THIS LINK TO CONTEXT?

ASK: DO OTHER QUOTATIONS LINK TO THIS?

[The telephone rings sharply]

FLASHCARD

TEAR THIS PAGE OUT, FILL THIS SIDE IN AND BINGO! YOU HAVE A FABULOUS FLASHCARD.

THIS QUOTATION IS FROM ACT _____.

THE WORDS BELONG TO _____

_____.

ONE LITERARY TECHNIQUE USED IS

_____.

ANOTHER LITERARY TECHNIQUE USED IS

_____.

THE WORD CLASS OF THE KEY WORD

" _____ " IS _____.

WRITE THE QUOTATION HERE — MAKE SURE IT IS <u>EXACTLY</u> THE SAME AS IT IS ON THE OTHER SIDE!

ASK: HOW DOES THIS MAKE YOU FEEL?
ASK: HOW WOULD OTHER AUDIENCES FEEL?
ASK: HOW DOES THIS LINK TO CONTEXT?
ASK: DO OTHER QUOTATIONS LINK TO THIS?

[As they stare guiltily and dumbfounded, the curtain falls]

FLASHCARD

TEAR THIS PAGE OUT, FILL THIS SIDE IN AND BINGO! YOU HAVE A FABULOUS FLASHCARD.

THIS QUOTATION IS FROM ACT _____ .

THE WORDS BELONG TO _____

_____ .

ONE LITERARY TECHNIQUE USED IS

_____ .

ANOTHER LITERARY TECHNIQUE USED IS

_____ .

THE WORD CLASS OF THE KEY WORD

" _____ " IS _____ .

WRITE THE QUOTATION HERE — MAKE SURE IT IS <u>EXACTLY</u> THE SAME AS IT IS ON THE <u>OTHER</u> SIDE!

ASK: HOW DOES THIS MAKE YOU FEEL?
ASK: HOW WOULD OTHER AUDIENCES FEEL?
ASK: HOW DOES THIS LINK TO CONTEXT?
ASK: DO OTHER QUOTATIONS LINK TO THIS?

Don't forget to photograph and share your doodles with your friends— they need the quotations too!

(Wear your best baseball hat and flares, obv.)

Pick your own quotation...

...and do a doodle to suit it.

FLASHCARD

TEAR THIS PAGE OUT, FILL THIS SIDE IN AND BINGO! YOU HAVE A FABULOUS FLASHCARD.

THIS QUOTATION IS FROM ACT _____ .

THE WORDS BELONG TO _____

_____ .

ONE LITERARY TECHNIQUE USED IS

_____ .

ANOTHER LITERARY TECHNIQUE USED IS

_____ .

THE WORD CLASS OF THE KEY WORD

" _____ " IS _____ .

WRITE THE QUOTATION HERE — MAKE SURE IT IS <u>EXACTLY</u> THE SAME AS IT IS ON THE OTHER SIDE!

ASK: HOW DOES THIS MAKE YOU FEEL?
ASK: HOW WOULD OTHER AUDIENCES FEEL?
ASK: HOW DOES THIS LINK TO CONTEXT?
ASK: DO OTHER QUOTATIONS LINK TO THIS?

Pick your own quotation...

...and do a doodle to suit it.

FLASHCARD

TEAR THIS PAGE OUT, FILL THIS SIDE IN AND BINGO! YOU HAVE A FABULOUS FLASHCARD.

THIS QUOTATION IS FROM ACT _____.

THE WORDS BELONG TO _____

_____.

ONE LITERARY TECHNIQUE USED IS

_____.

ANOTHER LITERARY TECHNIQUE USED IS

_____.

THE WORD CLASS OF THE KEY WORD

" _____ " IS _____.

WRITE THE QUOTATION HERE — MAKE SURE IT IS <u>EXACTLY</u> THE SAME AS IT IS ON THE OTHER SIDE!

ASK: HOW DOES THIS MAKE YOU FEEL?
ASK: HOW WOULD OTHER AUDIENCES FEEL?
ASK: HOW DOES THIS LINK TO CONTEXT?
ASK: DO OTHER QUOTATIONS LINK TO THIS?

Pick your own quotation...

...and do a doodle to suit it.

FLASHCARD

TEAR THIS PAGE OUT, FILL THIS SIDE IN AND BINGO! YOU HAVE A FABULOUS FLASHCARD.

THIS QUOTATION IS FROM ACT _____ .

THE WORDS BELONG TO _____

_____ .

ONE LITERARY TECHNIQUE USED IS

_____ .

ANOTHER LITERARY TECHNIQUE USED IS

_____ .

THE WORD CLASS OF THE KEY WORD

" _____ " IS _____ .

WRITE THE QUOTATION HERE — MAKE SURE IT IS <u>EXACTLY</u> THE SAME AS IT IS ON THE OTHER SIDE!

ASK: HOW DOES THIS MAKE YOU FEEL?
ASK: HOW WOULD OTHER AUDIENCES FEEL?
ASK: HOW DOES THIS LINK TO CONTEXT?
ASK: DO OTHER QUOTATIONS LINK TO THIS?

Pick your own quotation...

...and do a doodle to suit it.

FLASHCARD

TEAR THIS PAGE OUT, FILL THIS SIDE IN AND BINGO! YOU HAVE A FABULOUS FLASHCARD.

THIS QUOTATION IS FROM ACT _____.

THE WORDS BELONG TO _____

_____.

ONE LITERARY TECHNIQUE USED IS

_____.

ANOTHER LITERARY TECHNIQUE USED IS

_____.

THE WORD CLASS OF THE KEY WORD

" _____ " IS _____ .

WRITE THE QUOTATION HERE — MAKE SURE IT IS EXACTLY THE SAME AS IT IS ON THE OTHER SIDE !

ASK: HOW DOES THIS MAKE YOU FEEL?

ASK: HOW WOULD OTHER AUDIENCES FEEL?

ASK: HOW DOES THIS LINK TO CONTEXT?

ASK: DO OTHER QUOTATIONS LINK TO THIS?

Pick your own quotation...

...and do a doodle to suit it.

FLASHCARD

TEAR THIS PAGE OUT, FILL THIS SIDE IN AND BINGO! YOU HAVE A FABULOUS FLASHCARD.

THIS QUOTATION IS FROM ACT _____ .

THE WORDS BELONG TO _____

_____ .

ONE LITERARY TECHNIQUE USED IS

_____ .

ANOTHER LITERARY TECHNIQUE USED IS

_____ .

THE WORD CLASS OF THE KEY WORD

" _____ " IS _____ .

WRITE THE QUOTATION HERE — MAKE SURE IT IS <u>EXACTLY</u> THE SAME AS IT IS ON THE <u>OTHER</u> SIDE !

ASK: HOW DOES THIS MAKE YOU FEEL?
ASK: HOW WOULD OTHER AUDIENCES FEEL?
ASK: HOW DOES THIS LINK TO CONTEXT?
ASK: DO OTHER QUOTATIONS LINK TO THIS?

OF COURSE, NONE OF THIS IS ANY SUBSTITUTE FOR ACTUALLY SEEING THE PLAY (OR FILM)

O yes, and read it too.

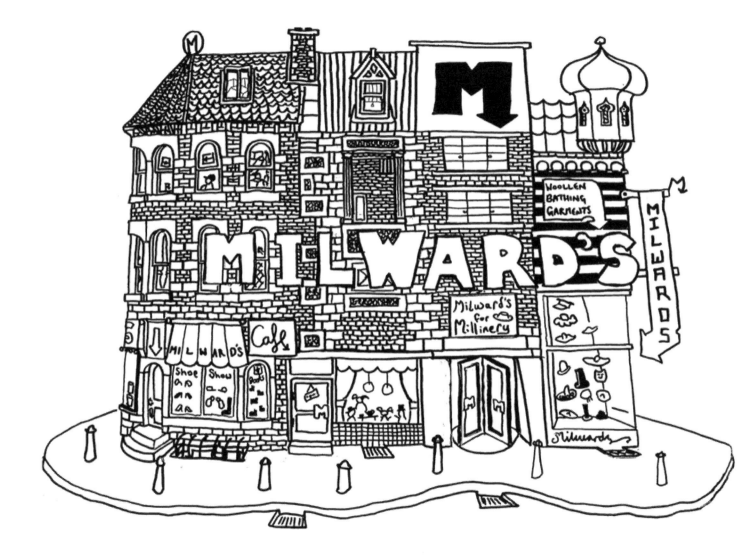

Printed in Great Britain
by Amazon